W9-ADG-033

Jones Library, Inc.
43 Amity Street
Amherst, MA 01002
WITHDRAWN

Science
and
Sustainable Agriculture

Patricia D. Netzley

San Diego, CA

© 2018 ReferencePoint Press, Inc.
Printed in the United States

For more information, contact:
ReferencePoint Press, Inc.
PO Box 27779
San Diego, CA 92198
www.ReferencePointPress.com

ALL RIGHTS RESERVED.
No part of this work covered by the copyright hereon may be reproduced or used in any form or by any means—graphic, electronic, or mechanical, including photocopying, recording, taping, web distribution, or information storage retrieval systems—without the written permission of the publisher.

LIBRARY OF CONGRESS CATALOGING-IN-PUBLICATION DATA

Name: Netzley, Patricia D., author.
Title: Science and Sustainable Agriculture/by Patricia D. Netzley.
Description: San Diego, CA: ReferencePoint Press, Inc., 2017. | Series:
   Science and Sustainability | Audience: Grades 9 to 12.
Identifiers: LCCN 2017016048 (print) | LCCN 2017025827 (ebook) | ISBN
   9781682822524 (eBook) | ISBN 9781682822517 (hardback)
Subjects: LCSH: Sustainable agriculture—Juvenile literature.
Classification: LCC S494.5.S86 (ebook) | LCC S494.5.S86 N477 2017 (print) |
   DDC 631.5—dc23
LC record available at https://lccn.loc.gov/2017016048

CONTENTS

The Role of Science

> **"Sustainable agriculture is grounded in the idea of steward-ship: preserving the resources that allow us to meet our own needs, so that future generations can meet theirs too."**
>
> —Union of Concerned Scientists
>
> Union of Concerned Scientists, "Solutions: Advance Sustainable Agriculture." www.ucsusa.org.

Beneath the High Plains of the United States is the largest supply of freshwater in the world: the Ogallala Aquifer (also sometimes referred to as the High Plains Aquifer), a 174,000-square-mile (450,658 sq. km) underground area of gravel, sand, clay, and silt that holds liquid the way a sponge would. Most of the aquifer's roughly 1 quadrillion gallons (3.8 quadrillion L) of water has been there for millions of years. The rest comes from rainfall, floodwater, and other water seeping down from above.

In the eight states that overlie the aquifer, nearly two hundred thousand wells have been drilled to bring the Ogallala's water to the surface, where it is used for drinking and irrigation. As a result, the aquifer provides roughly 30 percent of the irrigation ground-water for crops and livestock in the United States, watering nearly one-fifth of the country's corn, wheat, cotton, and cattle. But in order to meet this demand, the wells are pumping out more water than nature can replace—a practice that over the past fifty years has dropped the water level of the aquifer about 160 feet (49 m) on average.

This drop is not uniform across the aquifer because its water-saturated parts have different thicknesses. Some parts are as much as 1,000 (305 m) feet thick, while others are only a few feet. Wherever the aquifer is thinnest, wells can run dry. Such was the case in Happy, Texas, where wells that provided abundant water when they were drilled in the 1950s now no longer provide any water at all. This means that most people in the area can no longer grow crops or keep livestock, since it is too difficult and expensive for them to bring in water from elsewhere.

WORDS IN CONTEXT

aquifer
An underground geological formation that bears water.

Unsustainable Practices

Given the rate at which the Ogallala is being drained, scientists say, other towns will soon suffer the same fate as Happy, particularly in Kansas, Oklahoma, Nebraska, and parts of Colorado. In fact, eventually all of the aquifer will be dry. This means that the current approach to managing the Ogallala's resources is unsustainable. As David Brauer, an expert in soil and water management with the Agricultural Research Service of the US Department of Agriculture, reports, "The Ogallala supply is going to run out and the Plains will become uneconomical to farm. That is beyond reasonable argument."[1]

Moreover, because of how important the plains are to America's food supply, the drying up of the Ogallala will affect more than just the people living in towns above the aquifer. As health reporter Mike Adams notes, "Without the Ogallala Aquifer, America's heartland food production collapses. No water means no irrigation for the corn, wheat, alfalfa and other crops grown across these states to feed people and animals."[2]

Other unsustainable farming practices threaten food supplies as well. For example, mishandling the clearance of land can allow fertile topsoil to be blown away by winds or swept away by floods, and using pesticides carelessly can kill bees that pollinate fruit trees, which means that such trees will yield less or even no

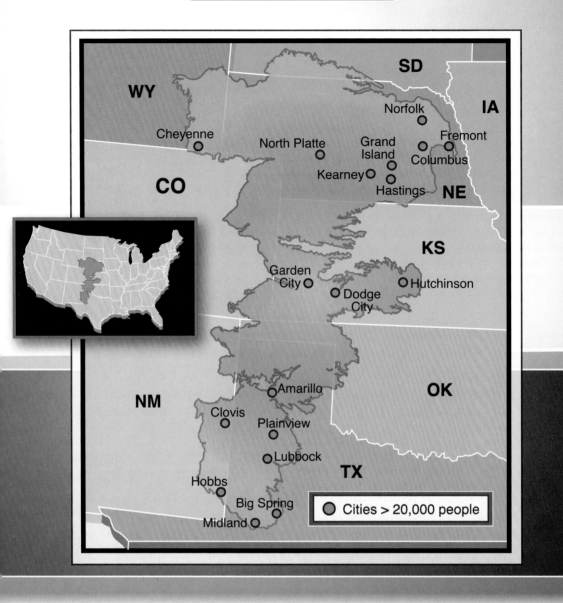

fruit. (Pesticides include herbicides, insecticides, and other chemicals that kill many of the most serious threats to food crops.)

Practices that adversely affect food production are particularly worrisome given that the world's population is growing. Experts say that the global population will likely be 9.2 billion by 2050 and that even if farmers can produce the same amount of food by then as they do today, there will not be enough for everyone. In fact, in order to have enough food, farmers will have to increase their crop yields by at least 70 percent.

Conventional Versus Sustainable Agriculture

Farmers disagree on how to attain this goal. Those who practice conventional agriculture believe it is paramount to produce the most crops possible in any given growing season. This approach to farming is often called industrial agriculture because it typically relies on mechanizing the growing, harvesting, and processing of food. To this end, such practitioners rely on the large-scale application of commercial fertilizers, herbicides, and pesticides to keep the soil and plants productive, irrespective of the risk these chemical products pose to the environment.

In contrast, farmers who practice sustainable agriculture believe that while it is important to produce as much food as possible, it is equally important to preserve the environment for future generations. Therefore, they focus on soil and plant management techniques that, although often requiring more time and care, make crops more resilient to pests and other threats. As the Agricultural Sustainability Institute of the University of California–Davis explains, "A common philosophy among sustainable agriculture practitioners is that . . . a healthy soil will produce healthy crop plants that have optimum vigor and are less susceptible to pests."[3]

This approach has proved to be highly successful for farmers willing to invest great care and patience in their endeavors. The Grace Communications Foundation, which seeks to raise awareness related to food production as it impacts the environment and public health, reports, "Sustainable crop production practices can lead to higher yields over time, with less need for expensive and environmentally damaging inputs."[4]

Vital Innovations

Scientists have aided the practitioners of sustainable agriculture by using controlled pollination and genetic engineering to develop new varieties of plants that can resist disease and/or pests without the need for chemical additives. For example, scientists have been attempting to create types of gourds and melons, such as cucumbers, pumpkins, and cantaloupe, that are resistant to a type of fungus known as mildew. Other research has focused on creating plants that can grow in soil that is too salty or too dry or that lacks certain nutrients. These plants require less water and fewer soil amendments in order to grow.

Scientific efforts related to sustainable agriculture are producing many other innovations as well. These include new types of pesticides, herbicides, and fertilizers that are less harmful to the environment, new approaches to crop and livestock management that improve soil and animal health, and new tools and technologies that make various aspects of farming more productive and cost efficient. In addition, scientists are working to combat the harmful effects of climate change, which brings such crises as droughts and floods.

Because of such challenges, many experts believe that sustainability science deserves more public support. Australia's chief scientist, professor Ian Chubb, for example, has argued that more funding should be made available for agricultural research and that more young people should be encouraged to go into agricultural science. He, like many, believes that "it's only through recognising the importance of science, invention and technology that we can possibly hope to guarantee a truly sustainable future."[5]

CHAPTER ONE

Science and the Sustainability Movement

> **"**Historical evidence traces an ebb and flow of concern for stewardship and long-term food production over the years. . . . It is not surprising that particularly difficult times and places spawned the most dramatic 'learning curves' in terms of both successful and failed practices and systems.**"**

—US Department of Agriculture

US Department of Agriculture, "Tracing the Evolution of Organic/Sustainable Agriculture," May 2007. www.nal.usda.gov.

Science related to sustainable agriculture has its roots in three ways of thinking about farming practices. The first considers farming in terms of food production, with the aim of providing enough food for a given population. The second considers farming in terms of how it affects the land, with the aim of developing ways for farmers to be good stewards of the environment. The third considers farming as a means to sustain the people living in rural communities, in terms of providing not just food but work and income.

Agronomy and Agroecology

One of the sciences that is key to sustainable agriculture is agronomy, which focuses on soil management and crop production. Much of agronomy involves selectively breeding plants in order to improve their nutritional value and to increase crop yields. One of the earliest and most prominent agronomists to do this kind of selective breeding was Nazareno Strampelli of Italy. When he began his work in 1900, the main crop for many Italian landowners was wheat, particularly varieties used for making bread. But these were tall varieties of wheat, which means they were susceptible to lodging—the collapse of a cereal plant stem that occurs when it can no longer hold its own weight. They were also susceptible to two conditions that can reduce yield: drought stress and stem rust, the latter of which is a fungal disease that damages plant stems. Strampelli spent forty years addressing these problems, crossbreeding plants in order to develop hardier plants with shorter stems. Largely as a result of this work, by 1935 Italy's overall wheat production had doubled.

While Strampelli was striving to increase yields, other scientists started looking at how the agricultural practices on a farm can affect the ecosystems around it. These scientists worked in the field of ecology—a branch of biology that deals with, among other things, how organisms interact with the environment. By the late 1920s this work had developed into another new scientific discipline, agroecology, which applied ecological methods to the study of agricultural issues.

> **WORDS IN CONTEXT**
>
> **agroecosystem**
> An agricultural area and the organisms within that area, considered as an ecosystem.

However, it was several more years before the field of agroecology began to gain significant notice as a field of study. This increased attention was due largely to the work of German ecologist and zoologist W. Tischler. His 1965 book, *Agroecology*, drew attention to his studies on how plants, animals, soils, and climate interacted within an agroecosystem, an ecosystem under agricultural management. By studying the ways in which farmers affect the soil, plants, animals, and land under their control, Tischler shed light on problems related to issues such as pest control, soil biology, and plant protection.

Such studies continue today. For example, a long-term agroecosystem research project in Nebraska is working to identify how

The science of agronomy involves soil management and crop production, both of which are essential to sustainable agriculture. One element of crop production, selective breeding, strives for healthier plants and higher crop yields.

farmers in that state are impacting their water resources. Specifically, scientists are looking into how crop, beef cattle, and grassland systems are affecting the Ogallala Aquifer and the Platte River.

New Ideas

Studies related to increasing crop yields also continue today. Much of this work has been built upon efforts in the 1950s and 1960s to use agricultural science to fight starvation. Such efforts took place in parts of Asia, Africa, and Latin America where farmers were unable to provide enough food for growing populations. The man at the forefront of these efforts was American biologist Norman Borlaug.

WORDS IN CONTEXT

crossbreeding

Breeding one type, variety, or species of plant or animal with another, different one.

Beginning in the 1940s in Mexico, Borlaug used crossbreeding over a period of many years to create tens of thousands of hardier wheat varieties. Their traits include a resistance to certain diseases, thicker stems (which can support more heads of grain), and an ability to adapt to and thrive in less-than-ideal environments (such as places where the soil is poor or the water sparse). The plants with thicker stems were also much shorter and more compact than normal, which meant that each of these highly productive plants took up less space in a field. In other words, farmers who planted these plants could produce more wheat on less land.

Borlaug also figured out a way to speed up his research into the fungal rust that attacks wheat. In the process, he developed a method for growing stronger, hardier, more adaptable plants. This all came about because a single season of growth did not provide Borlaug with enough plants for his research. To have crops available for study year round, he carried seeds from his summer crop in southern Mexico to the north in the winter and from his winter crop in northern Mexico to the south in the summer. No other plant breeder had ever done this before.

Borlaug's two-crops-a-year approach, which became known as shuttle breeding because the seeds were carried—or shuttled—from one place to another, doubled the pace of his research. It had other benefits as well. By being exposed to two different crop fields, the seeds had different characteristics than seeds that grew in just one field. Moreover, any plant that grew well in both places demonstrated it could adapt to different latitudes, altitudes, climates, rainfall amounts, soil conditions, oxygen levels, hours of daylight, and disease exposures. In other words, Borlaug's method of increasing the pace of his research also resulted in improved plants. He later reported, "Through the use of this technique, we developed high-yielding, day-length-insensitive varieties with a wide range of ecologic adoption and a broad spectrum of disease resistance—a new combination of uniquely valuable characters in wheat varieties."[6]

Greater Yields

Borlaug's improved plants and growing techniques led to great increases in crop yields in Mexico. Science writer Justin Gillis reports that "by the early 1960s, many farmers in Mexico had embraced the full package of innovations from Dr. Borlaug's breeding program, and wheat output in the country had soared sixfold from the levels of the early 1940s."[7] Mexican farmers could now

SELECTIVE BREEDING

Plants that provide food are very different today than they were centuries ago. This is largely because of human intervention. Farmers would come across a plant with superior qualities—perhaps its fruit was juicier or sweeter, for example. They would save the seeds of that plant to use the next time and the next, often continuing over many generations in a process known as selective breeding.

Experts say corn, or maize, is an example of just how dramatically selective breeding can change a plant over a long period of time. Beginning in the 1930s, a few scientists suspected that corn is related to a Mexican grass called teosinte, but most rejected this theory because teosinte is so unlike corn in appearance. (It has skinny ears, few kernels, and a hard casing instead of a husk.) Then in 2010 scientists found samples of ancient corn at an archaeological site in Mexico, performed more genetic testing, and confirmed that corn did indeed develop from teosinte. Of this discovery, scientist Sean B. Carroll says:

> The most impressive aspect of the maize story is what it tells us about the capabilities of agriculturalists 9,000 years ago. These people were living in small groups and shifting their settlements seasonally. Yet they were able to transform a grass with many inconvenient, unwanted features into a high-yielding, easily harvested food crop. The domestication process must have occurred in many stages over a considerable length of time as many different, independent characteristics of the plant were modified.

Sean B. Carroll, "Tracking the Ancestry of Corn Back 9,000 Years," *New York Times*, May 24, 2010. www .nytimes.com.

grow enough wheat to meet the needs of their own population as well as having enough left over for sale to other countries.

Also in the 1960s, Borlaug was able to expand the reach of his work to parts of Asia and the Middle East. This outreach began after the governments of India and Pakistan, facing dramatic rises in population and fearing widespread starvation, called on Borlaug to help them provide enough food for their people. He responded by providing farmers in both countries with seeds from his improved plants. In 1965, for example, he sent 200 tons (181

Norman Borlaug (pictured in 1970) compares wheat stalks that were grown at the Rockefeller Agricultural Institute in Mexico. Borlaug pioneered the development of high-yield grains and new irrigation and fertilization techniques.

metric tons) of semidwarf wheat seeds to India and 250 tons (227 metric tons) to Pakistan. The resulting crops produced the highest yields of wheat ever seen in either country.

In addition, Borlaug convinced the governments of both countries to invest in infrastructure related to irrigation and other aspects of food production. He also persuaded them to provide farmers with seeds and fertilizer and to promote agricultural practices that increase crop yields. Consequently, as in Mexico, yields increased dramatically. Science writer Henry I. Miller of *Forbes* magazine reports that in India, "by 1968, thanks to Borlaug's varieties, the wheat grew densely packed, was resistant to rust, and the maximum yield had risen to 6000 lbs per acre."[8]

Borlaug went on to contribute his expertise to farmers in other parts of the world. He was also instrumental in establishing research facilities that built on his work by improving not only wheat plants but other types of cereal grains as well. For example, some colleagues of Borlaug developed new rice varieties as compact as the semidwarf wheat that he had created. These highly productive rice plants quickly spread throughout much of Asia. Because of such work, according to Miller, by 1992 the world's grain output, in terms of yield per acre, had gone up more than 150 percent.

Moreover, Miller notes, Borlaug helped the environment as well. Miller explains, "Without high-yield agriculture, either millions would have starved or increases in food output would have been realized only through drastic expansion of land under cultivation— with losses of pristine wilderness far greater than all the losses to urban, suburban and commercial expansion."[9] Instead, although food production rose by 150 percent from the 1960s to 2008, the amount of forests and other wilderness areas converted to farms only increased by 10 percent.

The Green Revolution

Borlaug also played a major role in an agricultural movement known as the green revolution, which lasted from the 1930s to the 1960s. The movement's name refers to a series of worldwide initiatives led by Borlaug that transferred agricultural knowledge and technology from developed countries to developing ones.

During those years, agriculture throughout the world became dramatically more productive.

This productivity was not just due to the development of high-yield plants like Borlaug's wheat. It was also because of the creation of new types of chemical fertilizers and synthetic herbicides and pesticides. The fertilizers provided the plants with more nutrients, the herbicides controlled destructive weeds, and the pesticides warded off or eliminated insects and diseases. All of these things helped crops thrive.

Another feature of the green revolution was the implementation of a new farming technique known as multiple cropping. This is the practice of growing two or more types of crops on the same acreage in one growing season. There are several types of multiple cropping. Relay cropping, for example, involves planting a second crop immediately after the first one has been harvested, while row intercropping involves planting two or more crops at the same time within the same field but in different rows.

Multiple cropping ensures that a piece of farmland does not stand idle at any point within the growing season. However, plants are typically chosen carefully so that they will not be competing for the same resources in a particular piece of land. For example, in a two-crop field with row intercropping, one type of plant might have deep roots and the other shallow roots so that they are not accessing the same water.

By introducing these new ways to farm, as well as new types of plants, fertilizers, herbicides, and pesticides, the green revolution helped increase food production and prevent starvation. However, many small farmers in developing countries were unable to afford the costs of the revolution's innovations. The new plants and chemical products were more expensive than the plants and products these farmers were accustomed to using, and the new farming practices were often more labor intensive. It was also difficult for poor farmers to pay for improvements to their irrigation systems, and in drier areas the new irrigation techniques were typically impossible to implement. Similarly, some farmers were unable to learn the new water-management skills being promoted by green revolutionists.

IMPROVING FARMING METHODS

Calls for a new green revolution are typically calls for new technologies, particularly related to genetic engineering. But some experts say that more emphasis should be placed on improving agricultural methods. One such person is Jill Richardson, author of *Recipe for America: Why Our Food System Is Broken and What We Can Do to Fix It.* She argues that what is needed most is the widespread adoption of sustainable agroecological methods, along with economic and social reforms that will benefit not only farm owners but their workers as well. Moreover, she suggests that just because certain agricultural methods have been used for centuries does not mean they should be discarded as outdated. She explains: "Our ancestors lacked the science to understand why crop rotation, composting, and cover crops worked so well, but today we do. With the latest science and technology, we can improve upon the farming methods used by generations before us, without abandoning those methods entirely."

Jill Richardson, "Norman Borlaug's Unsustainable Green Revolution," Common Dreams, October 5, 2009. www.commondreams.org.

Scientists and others who promoted the green revolution were also instrumental in the expansion of herbicide and pesticide use in countries that previously had little experience with these chemicals. Herbicides and pesticides provided farmers with modern tools for fighting weeds and pests that could decimate their crops. But these chemicals had a huge downside: They often killed beneficial insects, and in many cases they also ended up in farm runoff that polluted sources of water used for drinking and irrigation. Moreover, direct contact with these herbicides and pesticides harmed the people who worked with them every day. A 2008 study by researchers at Punjabi University in India, for instance, discovered that 30 percent of Indian farmers who had been exposed to these herbicides and pesticides had damaged DNA (the substance in cells that carries genetic information).

Crop diversity was also negatively affected by green revolution practices. Farmers were encouraged to grow only those varieties of plants that would give them high yields. In India, for example, the majority of farmers now rely on just ten varieties of rice, whereas prior to the green revolution thirty thousand varieties of rice were grown in the country. Lack of genetic diversity leaves crops vulnerable to devastation by diseases and pest infestations.

A New Green Revolution

The harmful aspects of the green revolution made it unsustainable. But by studying these aspects, experts in agricultural science have been able to determine what must be avoided in order for a new green revolution to succeed. For example, many scientists say it is important to do a better job of helping poor farmers adopt sustainable practices so that the entire planet will play a part in any green revolution to come. In regard to this issue, the International Food Policy Research Institute—an organization dedicated to finding sustainable ways to end hunger and poverty—states, "Policymakers will

Farmers in some developing countries benefited from the seeds and techniques developed during the green revolution. But getting seeds and supplies to other farmers, such as those in Africa (pictured), proved difficult.

need to target the poor more precisely to ensure that poor people receive greater direct benefits from new technologies." The institute adds, "By building on the strengths of the Green Revolution while seeking to avoid its weaknesses, scientists and policymakers can take significant steps toward achieving sustainable food security for all the world's people."[10]

WORDS IN CONTEXT

pathogens

Microorganisms, including viruses and bacteria, that cause disease.

Indeed, many experts believe it is time for this kind of revolution, in large part because of changing climate conditions. They believe such changes will lead to new problems that can only be solved with the kind of scientific efforts that took place during the green revolution. For example, in speaking of the current high levels of crop productivity in California, Phillip A. Sharp and Alan Leshner, both of whom serve on the board of the Supporters of Agricultural Research Foundation, say:

> Maintaining this level of productivity has been quite a challenge in recent years and is likely to become more difficult over the next few decades as weather patterns, available water and growing seasons shift further and threats of invasive weeds, pests and pathogens rise. If agriculture is to have any chance of answering these challenges, we must have new and improved techniques and technologies. The problem is that agricultural innovation has not kept pace.[11]

Sharp and Leshner believe that in the United States the main reason for this lack of innovation is the fact that the government no longer puts a priority on agricultural research. They report that only 2 percent of the federal money spent on research and development as a whole is related to agriculture. This is insufficient, they say, because climate change could present the United States with a crisis similar to the Dust Bowl of the 1930s. During the Dust Bowl, droughts and the overplowing of land across the American prairies led to severe dust storms that destroyed farmland and damaged the economy.

Experts say that such droughts and soil erosion could happen again if the earth continues to heat up. (The earth has been warming for the past one hundred years, but the rate of increase over the past forty years has been unusually rapid.) With this threat in mind, Sharp and Leshner say, "Now more than ever, we need to embrace 21st-century science, fund it and turn it loose so we can develop better methods of putting food on the table. Our world is changing; the way we grow and produce food needs a much richer diet of scientific ingenuity to keep pace."[12]

Looking to the Future

Sharp and Leshner also note that when scientists obtain funding, they often produce valuable work. One such project, funded by the US Department of Agriculture's Climate Change Mitigation and Adaptation in Agriculture program, involves the development of varieties of corn that can cope with drought conditions. Corn is an important staple in many countries that also have experienced extreme drought. The lead researcher, Randall Wisser of the University of Delaware, reports, "Finding ways to efficiently adapt crops to new environments is a frontier of agricultural genetics research."[13]

Such work typically involves what is essentially a more sophisticated form of crossbreeding. Specifically, scientists transfer genes that carry certain traits from one organism into another. For example, genes that keep a fish from freezing in cold water might be transferred to a tomato plant to produce frost-resistant tomatoes. Other such efforts aim to increase yields, reduce the amount of water or pesticides needed, and improve the nutrition that a plant provides to the people who consume it.

While some of this work is controversial, many people believe that genetics is the key to future sustainability. As Richard Hamilton, an expert in agricultural genetics, says, "With modern genetics, increasing crop yields can provide more food, feed, fiber and fuels without necessarily increasing the need for land, water or fossil fuel. . . . Perhaps with the right funding and incentives, perennial grain crops that would not require sowing each year . . . might become a reality."[14] Indeed, most scientists agree that there are many discoveries waiting to be made in the field of plant biology as it relates to sustainable agriculture.

CHAPTER TWO

Promoting Biodiversity

> **"Biodiversity is important at all scales of the agricultural landscape. From billions of different soil microbes that help cycle nutrients and decompose organic matter, to wasps and bats that help reduce crop pests, to birds and insects that pollinate high value crops, biodiversity helps farmers successfully grow food and maintain sustainable farm landscapes."**
>
> —Grace Communications Foundation, an organization that advocates for sustainable alternatives to industrial food system practices
>
> Grace Communications Foundation, "Biodiversity," 2017. www.sustainabletable.org.

Of all the aspects of agriculture that can determine whether a particular agroecosystem is sustainable, biological diversity, or biodiversity, is among the most significant. *Biodiversity* is defined as the existence of a variety of life forms in an environment. An example of a biodiverse agroecosystem is a field planted with two types of crops—such as grains (which include wheat and barley) and legumes (which include peas, lentils, and beans)—or with two varieties of the same crop (such as two types of wheat) in the same field. Such a system makes the farm more sustainable because different types of plants react differently to diseases, drought, pests, and other threats to their health. This means that a farm lacking biodiversity—by having only one type of crop, for example—can be wiped out by a single disease, infestation, or weather-related event. Writer Sami Grover explains, "The more diverse the system, the better, because if one species gets hit by disease, famine or some other form of shock, there are other elements playing a similar role in the system that can pick up the slack. This is what is often referred to as resilience—the ability of a system to adapt and reorganize itself in the face of shocks."[15]

One of the most famous cases of a system collapsing because of its lack of resilience involves the potato. Cheap and easy to grow and slow to spoil, potatoes have long been a staple food in many parts of the world. In the early 1800s in Ireland, potatoes were the main (and often only) source of sustenance for 30 to 40 percent of the population. They were also an important moneymaker for Ireland's farmers in that one-third of the country's potato harvest was sold to England for use as cattle feed. However, Ireland had only one kind of potato—a white potato known as the Irish Lumper. (In contrast, there are approximately four thousand varieties of potatoes in the Andes of South America—which is the source of the potatoes that eventually made their way to the European continent and then to Ireland.)

With only one kind of potato, Ireland's most important crop lacked biodiversity. This had devastating consequences. In 1845 the country's potatoes developed a disease called blight, caused by a fungus-like microorganism called *Phytophthora infestans*. The spread of the blight killed nearly every potato crop in the country. Ireland's potato-growing system was unsustainable—and people began to starve. Thus began what became known in Ireland as the Great Famine (and elsewhere in the world as the Irish Potato Famine). By the time it ended seven years later, approximately 1 million of Ireland's people had died and another million had emigrated to escape starvation.

> ### WORDS IN CONTEXT
>
> **blight**
>
> A plant disease, especially one caused by a fungus.

Genetically Uniform Crops

Agroecosystems lacking biodiversity have become unsustainable in modern times as well. For example, in the southern United States in the 1970s, a fungus called *Bipolaris maydis* decimated

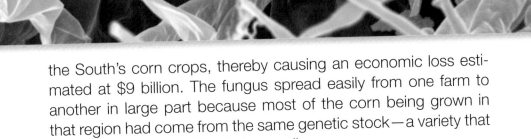

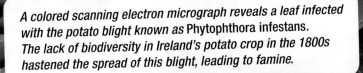
A colored scanning electron micrograph reveals a leaf infected with the potato blight known as Phytophthora infestans. The lack of biodiversity in Ireland's potato crop in the 1800s hastened the spread of this blight, leading to famine.

the South's corn crops, thereby causing an economic loss estimated at $9 billion. The fungus spread easily from one farm to another in large part because most of the corn being grown in that region had come from the same genetic stock—a variety that had no resistance to *Bipolaris maydis*.

In at least some of the affected farms, the fungus also might have been aided by plant crowding. Because genetically similar plants all tend to grow the same size and at the same rate, they can be planted closer together than plants that have different genetic traits. As Harvard University's Center for Health and the Global Environment reports, "Pathogens spread more readily, and epidemics tend to be more severe, when the host plants (or animals) are more genetically uniform and crowded. The pathogens encounter less resistance to spreading than they do in mixed stands."[16]

WORDS IN CONTEXT

monoculture

A crop made up of plants that are essentially identical to one another.

Another problem associated with monocultures—crops composed of plants that are essentially identical to one another—is that they are more susceptible to damage from insects. Experts have long known that monocultures attract more insect pests than fields growing a variety of crops. A study released in 2016 by the University of California–Davis supports this view. William Wetzel, an expert in population biology and the study's lead author, explains that insects go where they can find enough nutrients not just to survive but to thrive. If they encounter a field that is filled with one crop that suits that need, they will have no incentive to leave—or to leave anything behind. Wetzel explains, "A monoculture is like a buffet for plant-eating insects where every dish is delicious. A variable crop is like a buffet where every other dish is nasty."[17]

Genetic Modifications

Despite the problems that can arise with lack of crop diversity, many large farms prefer monocultures. This is because a uniform crop presents only one set of needs and problems, which makes planting and tending to the crop easier and more economical. More specifically, all of the plants can be planted, fertilized, watered, and harvested in the same way. And because they are all susceptible to the same pests and diseases, they can be treated with the same herbicides and pesticides—and at the same time. Moreover, plants tend to grow more robustly and uniformly when they are not competing with other species, and this improved growth often results in greater yields.

Given such benefits, many landowners who grow monocultures are loath to change their approach to farming. Because of this, scientists have been attempting to find ways to make monocultures less vulnerable to the problems they commonly experience. For example, experts in genetics have modified plant genes in order to develop varieties of corn that can resist certain insects and weeds and better tolerate drought.

There are currently 142 different types of genetically modified corn, making corn the most genetically modified plant species. In addition, roughly 90 percent of the corn, cotton, and soybeans grown in the United States today is genetically modified. Since the early 2000s, various types of genetically modified organisms (GMOs) have been grown on more than 2 billion acres (809 million ha) in twenty-eight countries.

In many cases, transforming an ordinary plant into a genetically modified plant begins with the selection of a donor

SUPPORTING BIODIVERSITY VIA FARM HABITATS

In trying to come up with ways to protect biodiversity, scientists have discovered that some kinds of farms, particularly those growing crops that require large amounts of water, can serve as good habitats for certain animal species. For example, researchers with the University of California–Davis and the nonprofit organization California Trout have discovered that rice fields are excellent places to raise young salmon. In fact, the fish raised in rice fields typically grow three times faster than those living in river channels and are larger in size upon reaching maturity. Moreover, upon maturity salmon raised in agricultural fields are typically able to find their own way to rivers, provided such a route exists (as is often the case in the agricultural areas of central California). Similarly, alfalfa fields have proved to be a good habitat for the Swainson's hawk, a bird listed as threatened according to California's Endangered Species Act, because such fields have the kinds of insects and rodents that the hawk likes to eat. Many other birds also find agricultural fields hospitable, given the right conditions. Several conservation groups are therefore working to teach farmers how to provide these conditions and/or improve existing bird-friendly habitats on their land.

organism—usually a bacterium, fungus, or plant. The donor organism is selected for traits that will benefit the plant the scientists want to modify. The scientists then identify which genes are carrying the desired traits and transfer this genetic material to the plant they are modifying. To make a genetically modified corn known as Bt corn, for example, scientists remove a gene from a soil bacterium called *Bacillus thuringiensis* (Bt). This bacterium produces a protein that kills the larvae of the European corn borer, a highly destructive caterpillar that chews through corn ears and stalks. (The tunnels they make through the stalks cause the plants to fall over.) Corn plants that are genetically modified with Bt are resistant to the borer.

WORDS IN CONTEXT

bacterium

One of a group of single-cell microorganisms (bacteria) that can cause disease.

Genetic modifications can also be made by altering genes within a particular plant so that they no longer function the way they did naturally. This has been the case, for example, with scientific research designed to find ways to keep foods from spoiling so quickly. In one such effort, scientists working with tomato plants 'turned off' certain genes associated with enzymes that affect when tomatoes start to ripen. As a result, tomatoes from the genetically modified plants remained firm for thirty days longer than those from unmodified plants.

Financial Sustainability

Genetic modifications that extend shelf life can make farms more sustainable via the economic benefits they confer. (A farm that consistently loses money is unlikely to survive.) Specifically, farmers are able to get more of their products to market, and those products are more desirable to consumers. Genetic modifications that make a plant resistant to certain insects and diseases can make a farm more financially sustainable as well. Those modifications can reduce or eliminate the need to subject plants to expensive herbicides and pesticides.

Once ripened, tomatoes quickly soften and spoil. Scientists have been able to genetically modify some tomato plants to keep the fruit firm for a longer period of time so that it remains fresh in stores.

However, the seeds that produce genetically modified plants—known as GMO seeds—are more expensive than unmodified seeds. This is largely because the companies that developed them control pricing, and there is little to no competition in the marketplace. In fact, just one company, Monsanto, produces eight of the ten GMO seeds that are commercially available in the United States. These eight are varieties of field corn, sweet corn, soybeans, cotton, alfalfa, sugar beets, canola, and squash. (The remaining two, developed by another company, are papaya and potato.)

Food Stability

Some experts believe that using GMO seeds is worth the added expense because, they say, the plants that grow from these seeds enhance a farm's sustainability. That is, genetically modified plants are more likely to thrive because they have a stronger resistance to certain serious threats. In fact, pro-GMO individuals argue that future world food supplies would be severely limited without plant research involving genetics. As Michael Keller of the International Seed Federation reports: "The seed industry continues to strive for improved and accessible seed with increased resistance to disease and pests, and an increased ability to withstand environmental extremes, in order to strengthen food security in the future."[18]

However, experts also acknowledge that genetically modified plants have the potential to threaten biodiversity. This can occur when pollens or seeds are carried by the wind or wildlife into natural environments. When this occurs, the growth of genetically modified plants can crowd out native plants or cross-pollinate with them, thereby eliminating the native species. Once the native plants disappear, bees and other pollinators that had been drawn to these plants can disappear as well. If this were to occur, many farms would be unsustainable, since one-third of all farm crops in the United States rely on pollination to reproduce. Consequently despite the benefits to farmers who use them, opponents argue that GMO seeds should not be used until, as the environmental organization Greenpeace states, there is "an adequate scientific understanding of their impact on the environment and human health."[19]

The Loss of Genetic Diversity

Native species can be supplanted just as easily by new varieties of plants that have been created using traditional breeding techniques as opposed to genetic modifications. Concerns over the effects of allowing traditionally bred plants to crowd out native ones have existed for decades, particularly in regions of the world where farmers rely on native species for their crops (because such plants are ideally suited for the local environment). In the 1940s Carl O. Sauer, who consulted on Norman Borlaug's work in Mexico as a representative of the Rockefeller Foundation (a charitable organization that provided a grant to support this work), wrote in a letter to the foundation:

A good aggressive bunch of American agronomists and plant breeders could ruin the native resources for good and all . . . by introducing U.S. forms [of plants] instead of working on the selection of ecologically adjusted native items. The possibilities of disastrous destruction of local genes are great. . . . Mexican agriculture cannot be pointed toward standardization on a few commercial types without upsetting native economy and culture hopelessly.[20]

In other words, Sauer worried that US-bred plants introduced into Mexican farming communities threatened native species that might be better suited to farming there. Sauer was also concerned about the sustainability of Mexico's farms—and its economy and culture—once the native plants disappeared.

THE LOSS OF BEES

Scientists consider bees to be vital to biodiversity because by spreading pollen from plant to plant, these insects enable many plants to reproduce. In fact, over 80 percent of plant species depend on pollinating insects, especially bees, to produce fruit and seeds. This means that bees are vital to sustainable agriculture as well—since without fruit, for example, there is no fruit harvest.

Consequently scientists and farmers are extremely concerned about decreases in bee populations. The Center for Biological Diversity recently evaluated the population of bees in North America and Hawaii. According to its February 2017 report, more than seven hundred species of bees are in decline, and one out of four native bee species are under threat of extinction. The main cause of this decline, the report says, is agriculture, most notably in regard to the destruction of native habitats and the use of pesticides. The report also notes that two of the most important US farming regions, California's Central Valley and the Corn Belt of the Midwest, are among those places with the lowest number of wild bees. The report states that "immediate action is needed if we are going to stop the widespread decline of native bees."

Kelsey Kopec and Lori Ann Burd, "Pollinators in Peril," Center for Biological Diversity, 2017. www.biological diversity.org.

More recently, some experts have become concerned that certain kinds of genetically modified plants might be driving all other kinds of life from their fields. One place where this might have occurred is a 600-acre (243 ha) Iowa farm growing genetically modified corn. During a visit to the farm, science writer and National Public Radio contributor Craig Childs observed only a handful of insects among the plants. He reports, "It felt like another planet entirely. I listened and heard nothing, no birds, no clicks from insects. There were no bees. The air, the ground, seemed

Some experts worry that bees and other pollinators might suffer if native plants are crowded out by the spread of genetically modified plants. Any loss in bee populations is a worry because many crops rely on pollination for production.

vacant. Yet, 100 years ago, these same fields, these prairies, were home to 300 species of plants, 60 mammals, 300 birds, hundreds and hundreds of insects."[21]

Protecting Biodiversity

Scientists have yet to determine why a loss of this magnitude has occurred in this field and others like it. However, many fear what it might mean for the earth's biodiversity if farmers increasingly plant genetically modified crops. In fact, fears related to the potential loss of biodiversity in connection with such crops has caused nearly forty countries to forbid their farmers to grow genetically modified plants. Consequently, experts have been developing ways to prevent modified plants from getting out of control. For example, to prevent genetically modified plants from crossbreeding with native plants, scientists are working to make GMO seeds sterile or otherwise unable to reproduce in uncontrolled situations. A similar project involves making genetically modified plants unable to pass along their modifications if they do reproduce. Other scientists are working to create genetically modified plants that cannot survive unless they are regularly provided with a substance, such as a synthetic version of an amino acid, that does not exist in the wild.

If successful, this work will do much to protect native species. Of course, there is no way to save species that have already been lost to monocultures—and farmers' eagerness to embrace the use of commercial crop varieties, which are typically genetically uniform, has hastened such extinction. According to the Food and Agriculture Organization of the United Nations, since 1900, the year commercial crop varieties first became available, roughly 75 percent of plant genetic diversity has been lost. Therefore, experts say it is vital to convince farmers that it is in their best interest—and the planet's best interest—to adopt agricultural practices that promote biodiversity.

CHAPTER THREE

Fighting Pests

> **"Without the use of crop protection products, overall food production would decline, and many of the fruits and vegetables we enjoy in the store would be in short supply."**
>
> —Farmer Jennifer Dewey Rohrich of Rohrich Farms in North Dakota
>
> Quoted in Food Journal and Food, Nutrition & Science, "Why Do Farmers Spray Chemicals on Crops?," March 12, 2015. www.foodnutritionscience.com.

Farmers have battled agricultural pests—weeds, insects, fungi, parasites, and rodents—for centuries. Over time, scientists have developed numerous methods that farmers can use to control pests. Pesticides are probably the most widespread form of pest control. However, for a variety of reasons, agriculture that depends on pesticides is not considered to be sustainable. Overuse of pesticides can eventually cause certain pests to develop resistance. Another problem is that pesticides kill beneficial insects and plants along with harmful ones. Still another is that they can contaminate the environment, including water sources, and harm human health. Consequently, scientists and farmers have been searching for safer and more sustainable means of protecting valuable crops.

The Armyworm Threat

Much of the attention of pest-control researchers has been focused on threats to major food crops, particularly corn—and armyworms are among the most serious of these threats. In their larval form (that is, as caterpillars), armyworms can raze crops to the ground, moving across fields in large numbers to devour leaves and the reproductive parts of plants. Corn crops are a favorite food of armyworms, but one species, the fall armyworm, is known to eat nearly one hundred different types of plants.

In addition to being voracious, armyworm caterpillars are experts at hiding. Feeding only at night, they conceal themselves during the day under stones, clods of dirt, clumps of grass, or deep within corn husks and the whorls of leaves along the cornstalk. After about three weeks of gorging, the caterpillars dig down into the soil to await their transformation into moths. Once these moths emerge, they are ready to lay masses of eggs on the leaves or crowns of crops or on weeds and grasses at the edges of crop fields. When these eggs hatch five to ten days later, the feeding frenzy begins again. Entomologist Georg Goergen, an expert on the species, reports that fall armyworms are "the number one pest of the Americas."[22] According to Centro Internacional de Mejoramiento de Maíz y Trigo (CIMMYT), or International Center for Improvement of Corn and Wheat, an organization involved in efforts to support sustainable corn and wheat farming, financial losses from fall armyworm activity in the United States alone in some years have reached as high as $297 million. Armyworms are also doing damage in parts of Africa and are expected to spread throughout that continent and reach Asia and the Mediterranean soon as well.

> **WORDS IN CONTEXT**
>
> **entomologist**
>
> A scientist who is an expert on insects.

The armyworm poses a serious threat to the world's food supplies largely because all species are extremely difficult to eradicate. This is due not just to their ability to hide but also because they breed very rapidly. Experts have found as many as six generations of fall armyworm eggs (roughly fifty eggs) in a single location. One species of armyworm that is native to Africa can achieve densities as concentrated as one thousand caterpillars per square meter.

Moreover, armyworms can be hard to kill with pesticides. According to the Food and Agriculture Organization of the United

The fall armyworm (pictured) poses a serious threat to food supplies worldwide. Scientists have been working with farmers to develop sustainable methods of ridding their crops of this destructive worm.

Nations, "The pest is known to cause extensive crop losses of up to 73 percent depending on existing conditions and is difficult to control with a single type of pesticide."[23] In part this is because fall armyworms quickly become resistant to a pesticide if it is used too often.

Chemical Resistance

Many pests—whether they are insects, animals, fungi, or weeds—can develop a resistance to chemical pesticides. In fact, more than five hundred species of insects, spiders, and mites have developed some degree of pesticide resistance. Moreover, resistances to toxins can build up relatively quickly. For example, the two-spotted spider mite, which sucks the fluids from the leaves of more than eleven hundred plant species, can develop a resistance within just two years of being introduced to a new pesticide. This mite is therefore resistant to many different types of pesticides.

The mechanism behind pesticide resistance is the fact that traits can be inherited. Specifically, when a particular insecticide, for example, is used repeatedly to fight a particular species, any individual insect that survives this assault might then pass along the ability to its offspring. With time and subsequent generations, the number of resistant insects grows to the point that an infestation can no longer be controlled using the same insecticide or others of its class.

Experts have also noted that certain insects appear to be developing a tolerance to toxin proteins that have been genetically added to corn plants to make the plants themselves toxic for insects that eat them. In Iowa and Brazil, for example, scientists have found rootworms and corn leaf worms thriving in fields of such corn. Consequently, they have advised farmers to alternate planting fields of genetically modified corn with unmodified corn in hopes of avoiding large-scale crop destruction.

Other Unintended Consequences

Efforts to eradicate armyworms vary by country. In the United States, for example, efforts to eradicate armyworms often involve a combination of pesticides, traps, and planting configurations that help minimize the damage of infestations. In other places in the world, pesticides are the primary means of dealing with armyworms. For example, in 2016 and 2017 governments of African countries began using military planes to spray chemical pesticides on thousands of acres of armyworm-infested crops.

Such widespread use of pesticides has consequences beyond the buildup of resistance. Many types of pesticides kill beneficial insects along with the intended targets. Bees are an important beneficial insect, but they are not the only one. Ground beetles, for instance, are voracious predators of slugs, snails, cutworms, cabbage maggots, and other pests that live in the soil. Ladybugs eat aphids, mites, and mealybugs. Lacewings eat aphids, caterpillars, mealybugs, scales, thrips, and whiteflies. Sustainable farming makes use of beneficial insects for pest control. But pesticides do not distinguish between harmful and beneficial insects. Most of the time, insects that come in contact with pesticides die. Sometimes insects even die from indirect contact with pesticides.

A ladybug devours aphids, one of its favorite meals. Pesticides kill insects that destroy crops but also kill beneficial insects, including ladybugs, lacewings, and ground beetles.

One commonly used class of insecticide that is particularly efficient at killing pests—and beneficial insects—is neonicotinoids, or neonics for short. This insecticide is applied to seeds so that it becomes incorporated into plants as they grow. When neonics are used, scientist Jennifer Sass says, "The plants become poison not only for the insects that farmers are targeting, but also for beneficial insects like bees."[24]

There have been many documented cases of neonics harming insects they were not intended to harm. In 2015 in Lewisburg, Pennsylvania, farmers observed a large number of ground beetle deaths. Ground beetles are an important predator of slugs—and slugs are voracious eaters of soybean plants. When the beetle die-off occurred, the farmers noticed a large increase in the number of slugs feeding on soybean plants.

> **WORDS IN CONTEXT**
>
> **neonics**
>
> Short for *neonicotinoids*, a class of insecticide that targets an insect's nervous system in order to kill it.

Scientists subsequently discovered that the beetles had not eaten the toxin-containing plants, which had been grown from neonic-coated seeds. The beetles had only eaten the slugs. But the slugs had fed on the soybean plants and continued to harbor the toxin inside their bodies, immune to its effects. This meant that if any other creature ate the slugs, it would have suffered the same fate as the beetles.

There is no evidence of any other animals having died from these slugs, but there is evidence of birds being killed by eating earthworms—which store toxins the way slugs do—that had consumed neonics. There is also evidence that neonics can remain in the soil for several years, which means that any plant that happens to grow in that soil might absorb the toxin and adversely affect anything that feeds on it. Therefore, some people have expressed the fear that neonics might ultimately cause widespread harm to biodiversity and sustainability, and some states and countries have permanently or temporarily banned the use of the pesticide.

New Products

Because of the threats that chemical pesticides can pose to human health, ecosystems, food sources, and sustainable agriculture, scientists have been working to come up with alternative products that are just as effective in controlling pests. Much of this work is related to nonsynthetic biological pesticides, or biopesticides. Biopesticides are derived from animal, plant, bacterial, mineral, or other natural materials and have been used in households and gardens for many years. (For example, baking soda, which can kill certain insects that are harmful to plants, is commonly used to kill ants that have invaded a home and aphids that have infested rose bushes.) But scientists are seeking to discover and develop new types of biopesticides that can be used to fight serious crop infestations.

WORDS IN CONTEXT

biopesticides

Pesticides derived from animal, plant, bacterial, mineral, or other natural materials.

As an example of these efforts, scientists working in Africa to combat armyworms have found that certain biopesticides can kill these insects. However, scientist Kenneth Wilson, who has been involved in this research, says that a product resulting from the work would be difficult to make and sell to farmers. He explains, "Biopesticides tend to be effective against a much narrower range of species than chemicals, which is good for the environment. But it means that they can only be used for a limited number of pests, often making them more expensive than chemicals."[25]

Consequently, some scientists are concentrating their efforts on developing a genetic technology called RNA interference that can alter the genes in pests in ways that make it impossible for them to survive. For example, in 2016 scientists developed an RNA spray fungicide to fight a disease-causing fungus that attacks barley plants. After the fungal cells absorb the spray, their genes are altered so that the fungus can no longer grow.

The company developing RNA sprays for commercial markets, Monsanto, says that the sprays only affect the targeted pest and do not linger in the environment. However, Doug Gurian-

Sherman, an expert in plant pathology and biotechnology with the Center for Food Safety, says the product is too new to know whether this is true. He states, "It is really impossible to predict all the things that could go wrong. That does not mean we should be paranoid about them, but we should be at least reasonably cautious and skeptical about claims of both safety and efficacy, since there is little experience or research to rely on."[26]

Using Predators to Kill Pests

Experts in sustainable agriculture recognize that sometimes farmers have no choice but to use pesticides to protect valuable crops. But many experts also believe that it is better to rely on natural means to combat pests. There are a variety of practices that can reduce crop damage while still allowing farms to make a profit. For example, when a field is standing idle—such as between a fall harvest and the end of winter—a farmer can plant other foliage there that will attract beneficial insects. This is often done to draw ground beetles to fields that will later be used to grow soybeans, so that these fields will have fewer slugs.

HIGHER COSTS, LESS APPEAL

Alternatives to pesticides—including hand-weeding fields and rotating crops—are more labor intensive than spraying pesticides or planting pesticide-treated seeds. More labor costs farmers more money. Consequently, the produce that comes from farms that rely on sustainable farming techniques typically costs more than produce that comes from farms that do not use these techniques. These increased costs are usually passed on to consumers. Produce from farms that use little or no pesticides can also look less appealing, because pests often cause fruit and vegetables to have blemishes, bruises, holes, or other marks.

This means that in the grocery store, a bruised apple, for example, can cost more than an unbruised one. Therefore, proponents of sustainable agriculture say that one of the keys to encouraging the spread of more environmentally friendly means of pest control will be to convince consumers that a piece of fruit does not have to look perfect to taste good.

Farmers can also turn to natural predators to combat pests. For example, in Thailand a type of wasp that kills mealybugs has been released in fields of cassava plants, which are a favorite food of the destructive mealybugs. Scientists researching ways to combat armyworm infestations have also been experimenting with this approach, trying to find natural predators that are up to the challenge of keeping fields armyworm-free. So far they have identified over a dozen species of parasitic wasps and several kinds of flies, viruses, and fungi that can kill armyworm larvae.

Using biological weapons like these is a key component to an ecosystem-based approach to sustainable farming known as integrated pest management (IPM). Another component of IPM involves monitoring insect populations in hopes of catching an infestation early—before it spins out of control. Often this involves weekly use of sweep nets to capture insects in a field for examination. By taking insect samples from various parts of a field, the farmer can determine just how seriously the crops are infested and by exactly which pests in which locations. Farmers might also walk the fields to examine individual plants for insects and related damage.

Once a farmer spots the beginnings of an infestation, he or she might spray an entire field with pesticides. However, IPM experts advocate applying pesticides only to the plants that are affected. They do this with spot-spraying methods or by placing bait stations (which hold substances that attract and kill certain kinds of insects) in infested parts of a field. In this way, the farmer avoids killing all insects in a field, which means beneficial insects are still able to keep populations of harmful insects in check and/or pollinate crops.

Yet another component of IPM is changing conditions in a field to reduce the chances that the field will harbor pests. For example, pruning plants regularly with sanitized shears to cut away diseased portions often prevents the spread of disease. The use of steam to sterilize soil can also be an effective strategy, because superheated steam can destroy certain kinds of pests. Tilling the soil periodically (that is, turning it over and breaking it up to eliminate soil compaction) can interrupt insect and rodent breeding, and not overwatering can prevent root diseases. And putting

Push-Pull Intercropping

Intercropping is a pest-control technique used in sustainable agriculture. It does not rely on harmful pesticides. Intercropping involves the planting of three crops: the desired crop; a second crop that repels, or pushes away, a targeted insect; and a third crop that attracts, or pulls in, the targeted insect. This is known as push-pull intercropping. It works like this: A farmer wishes to grow corn. But corn attracts a moth, whose larvae destroy the plants by tunneling through the stalks and ears. So between the rows of corn, the farmer plants desmodium—a legume that naturally repels the moths. On the outside border, the farmer plants Napier grass—which has a naturally occurring chemical that attracts the moths. The plants along the outside border attract the moths and the plants closest to the corn repel them—with the result that the corn can grow free of interference from the destructive moths.

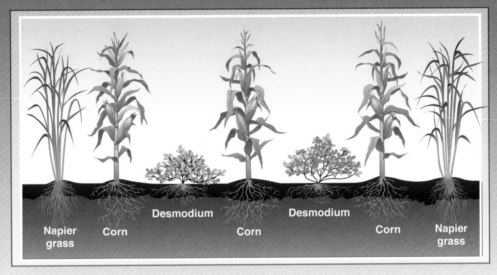

Source: Global Food Security, "Push-Pull." www.foodsecurity.ac.uk.

screens over plants or setting traps can keep away animals that would damage crops.

IPM has been widely embraced in the United States by those who practice sustainable agriculture. International organizations like CIMMYT have been promoting it in other countries as well. In fact, Martin Kropff, the director general of CIMMYT, says that in response to the armyworm threat in Africa, researchers "must be deployed to design and develop an integrated pest management strategy, which can provide sustainable solutions to effectively tackle the adverse effects of the fall armyworm."[27]

Planting Practices

Certain planting methods can also reduce the need for pesticides. One such method involves rotating crops. With crop rotation, farmers avoid planting the same crop in the same field year after year. By changing crops, farmers essentially fool insects that return for their favorite meal only to find it is no longer there. Without food the insects die—or move on to another location. Crop rotation also prevents diseases from gaining strength and plaguing crops year after year. The nonprofit organic farming organization Navdanya tells of one rice farmer in Dehradun, India, who has been able to grow rice, wheat, and corn without using any chemical pesticides for more than a decade simply by rotating these three crops.

Another practice that can reduce pesticide use is intercropping. With this approach, two or more small crops are planted between rows of the farmer's main crop in the same field. The purpose of

GETTING RID OF PESTS WITH SUPERHEATED STEAM

Soil sterilization involves treating agricultural soil in a way that will free it of bacteria, fungi, viruses, weeds, and other living organisms. Some farmers accomplish this by subjecting the soil to various chemicals, but practitioners of sustainable agriculture typically advocate the use of methods involving heat instead. (Extreme heat can kill living organisms.) On some farms, this might mean laying black plastic sheeting over the land and leaving it there for months of hot weather, so that the sun's rays can bake the soil that is under the plastic and therefore bake the organisms as well.

On other farms, various types of steaming equipment might be used to subject surface soil in a field or greenhouse to superheated steam. For example, a piece of equipment called a steaming hood, consisting of a steel or aluminum hood plus a boiler, can be towed across a field in order to cover the soil section by section so that each section can be subjected to steam. The length of time for this treatment varies according to the pests being targeted, the characteristics of the soil, and the depth of sterilization desired. However, for surface soil the range of time is most commonly five to twenty-five minutes. Farmers who do this then cover the soil with a sheet of some kind to retain the heat.

these small crops, often called intercrops or trap crops, is to draw certain pests away from a farmer's main crop. For example, in Kenya many farmers grow a variety of corn (their main crop) with two types of cereal crops (their intercrops). The cereal crops divert the attention of pests that commonly plague corn crops, such as corn borers, away from the corn crop and are attractive enough to keep the pests from returning to the corn.

Such practices are particularly important in poor countries, where farmers often cannot afford commercial pesticides. But farmers who can afford these products are increasingly adopting more sustainable practices as well. For many, this decision is based on their desire to safeguard their land for the farmers who will come after them. As South Dakota farmer Jennifer Dewey Rohrich says:

> We are a third generation farm and want to continue striving to preserve the land quality for our future generations. This wouldn't be possible if we abused the resources allowed to us. If farmers were to overuse things such as crop protection products, this could hurt their land. Bad, toxic, or depleted soil doesn't grow crops. We rely on the health and safety of our land in order to continue farming each year.[28]

In other words, many farmers try not to overuse pesticides. Many are also open to altering their farming methods. They are willing to adopt practices and products that will make their fields healthier and their agroecosystem more sustainable.

CHAPTER FOUR

Livestock Practices

> **"Consumers are now demanding more sustainable and ethically sourced food, including production without negative impacts on animal welfare, the environment and the livelihood of poor producers."**
>
> —Biologist and professor of animal welfare Donald Broom of the University of Cambridge
>
> Quoted in University of Cambridge, "Sustainable Livestock Production Is Possible," September 25, 2013. www.cam.ac.uk.

Worldwide, more than 60 billion animals per year are raised for human consumption, which means that livestock takes up a significant amount of space on the planet. Indeed, according to the Global Forest Coalition—an organization dedicated to protecting and restoring forest ecosystems—animals raised for meat and dairy production use 30 percent of Earth's land surface and 70 percent of all agricultural land. Consequently, practices related to livestock production have a significant impact on the environment. For example, providing animals with grazing land can result in the destruction of forests (deforestation), soil erosion, and a reduction of biodiversity. Transporting livestock and feed can cause air pollution via the vehicles used. Improperly handling animal waste can lead to groundwater contamination or other forms of water pollution. As a result, experts like biologist and professor of animal welfare Donald Broom of the University of Cambridge report that "many widely-used livestock production methods are currently unsustainable."[29]

Scientists concerned about sustainability as it pertains to livestock production have been working with farmers around the world to improve their animal-related practices, not just for the benefit of the land but for the benefit of the animals as well. These efforts vary widely because people in different parts of the world have different ideas about how animals should be treated and used. For example, in undeveloped countries, animal waste is considered a vital part of a farm because it provides organic matter than can maintain soil structure and prevent erosion. In contrast, in developed countries many farmers have traditionally considered animal waste to be an environmentally hazardous nuisance, although that attitude is slowly changing. Some of these farmers are reusing animal waste to fertilize their crops. Others are collecting manure, extracting methane gas from it, and using that gas to power generators to provide electricity for their farms.

Cleaning Up Manure

Even so, pollution caused by animal waste is of growing concern in the United States because of the increasingly common practice of keeping animals in confined-animal feeding operations, also known as factory farms. In such places dozens, hundreds, or perhaps thousands of animals are housed in quarters too small for their size and number rather than being allowed to graze. This practice reduces financial cost because it requires less land and makes animal care more efficient.

But it has another cost in terms of the environment. One of the results of factory farming is that livestock waste does not naturally decompose and become part of the soil, as it does when animals graze on open land. This creates a massive amount of animal waste. For example, in the United States alone, farm animals produce more than 335 million tons (304 million metric tons) of manure per year. And all of this manure has to be disposed of in a way that does not pollute the land and water.

In a typical scenario that involves dairy cows, for example, the animals live in buildings with slatted floors. The waste falls through the slats, where it is scraped or flushed with water and channeled into gutters that lead to a storage area. There this

Manure is collected from a large cow barn. After the manure is loaded into huge tanks, methane gas will be extracted from it and used to power a generator that provides electricity. This is one of many sustainable livestock practices developed by scientists and farmers working together.

mixture of water, urine, and feces—a liquid manure known as slurry—remains until it can be moved elsewhere for storage or disposal.

Many farmers treat and reuse the waste to fertilize crops. Reuse is usually a central goal of sustainable practices, but the methods for doing this can lead to environmental problems. Some farms channel the waste to settling basins, where solid and liquid waste are separated and then fed into manure lagoons. Within the lagoons, the manure is treated to eliminate odor and bacteria and other germs so that it can be used as fertilizer. Manure naturally contains a variety of bacteria, as well as viruses and other microorganisms, and scientists have worked to develop ways to combat these. For example, in the early 2000s researchers discovered that sodium carbonate, which is a mineral used in many laundry detergents, can reduce the amount of or even kill the E. coli bacteria present in cattle manure. (These bacteria can cause intestinal infections in humans.)

WORDS IN CONTEXT

manure lagoon
A human-made earthen basin lined with clay or a synthetic material, used to hold liquid manure.

Environmental Accidents

Manure also contains nitrogen, an element that all living things need in order to survive. When added to soil it can make plants grow faster, but in excess it can combine with chemicals like ammonia to create nitrate, a chemical compound that can kill fish if it finds its way into waterways. It can kill or sicken other animals as well, and there is evidence that nitrates can cause long-term health problems, including cancers, in humans.

Consequently, if excessive rainfall makes a lagoon overflow, or if for some other reason the stored liquid manure spills into the environment, it can have disastrous results. An example of such a disaster occurred one night in February 2016 in Fennimore, Wisconsin. As a portable pump set up by a local dairy farm was moving liquid manure from a full 3.3-million-gallon (12.5 million L) storage lagoon to a relatively new storage pit, the hose came loose and no one was there to see it. As a result, the manure began spilling out onto a highway and down a hill. Over the next few hours, its downward course took it on a 2-mile (3.2 km) journey to a creek. Later the owner of the dairy farm estimated that between 30,000 and 120,000 gallons (113,562 and 454,249 L) of manure had entered the water (although others said it could have been many times that).

Because of this accident, hundreds of trout at the popular Castle Rock Creek fishing spot died, and fresh water had to be pumped into the creek to save it from permanent damage. In addition, local residents were warned not to drink groundwater from nearby wells until it could be tested and treated for contamination. And although experts later restocked the creek with thousands of hatchling fish, it will be years before these trout have grown big enough to make catching them worthwhile.

There have been many such accidents over the years. In 2010, for example, a break in a berm (an earthen barrier) at a Washington State dairy farm led to 15 million gallons (57 million L) of manure and other waste being spilled into a slough that led to the Snohomish River. In July 2012 manure flowed for nearly three days from an Illinois pig farm into a nearby creek, killing all of its many fish. Two years later, despite a massive cleanup effort, studies of the area showed that nine species of fish that had once thrived there were no longer in evidence. And in 2016 in Iowa, a failed hose connection during a manure application—whereby manure is distributed over a field to fertilize crops—caused a spill that ended up in a nearby creek.

Not Enough Storage

There have also been cases of farmers intentionally dumping manure. According to news reports, one such incident took place over a period of a few weeks in 2009 in central Illinois. In this incident a pig farm owner pumped more than 27,000 gallons (102,206 L) of manure from his storage pits into an irrigation tank. Using a tractor, he then dragged the tank to the top of a slope and released its contents into a ravine. From there it flowed into a neighbor's cattle-watering pond and a creek, killing about 1,650 pounds (748 kg) of fish.

In an attempt to prevent this kind of pollution, local and state governments have enacted laws related to how manure should be handled and how much can be discharged at once. In addition, the US government requires nearly all concentrated animal feeding operations to apply for a permit if they are planning to discharge waste in streams, rivers, or lakes. The US Environmen-

A farmer spreads manure fertilizer on a field. Some dairy farms that have excess manure participate in programs known as manure shares. These programs match farms with anyone who wants manure to fertilize their plants.

tal Protection Agency (EPA) can prosecute people who discharge animal waste illegally. However, prosecution is rare, and fines are usually relatively small. After pleading guilty to misdemeanor criminal waste disposal, the Illinois pig farmer was fined $500.

Unsustainable practices contributed to the pig farmer's problems with waste storage. According to news reports of the incident, he had six hundred hogs, which produced more than 2 million pounds (907,185 kg) of manure per year, and not nearly enough storage space on his property. Such insufficiencies are not unusual, but farmers have other options for disposing of waste. One option is to pay a waste disposal company to legally remove the waste. Still, as experts point out, this practice typically cannot be sustained over the long run because it is costly. Moreover, the heavy trucks used to do this job eat up a lot of fuel—which adds pollutants to the atmosphere.

Sustainable Options

Many farmers who want to remove manure from their property try to find nearby farmers willing to take the waste to use as fertilizer for their crops. This is particularly important for dairy farmers, because more than 50 percent of the milk in the United States is produced by dairy farms with more than one thousand cows. The largest dairy farms have fifteen thousand or more cows, and dairy cows produce more waste than any other farm animal—including beef cattle. In fact, the EPA has determined that the average amount of manure produced daily by two thousand dairy cows is 240,000 pounds (108,862 kg), or nearly 90 million pounds (41 million kg) a year.

Because manure from dairy cows, in particular, is a good natural fertilizer, it can be used on a variety of plants. In addition to adding nutrients to the soil, it adds organic matter that improves soil structure, aeration, water permeability, and moisture-holding capacity. For this reason, many dairy farmers are able to give away or sell manure rather than storing or dumping it. In Brown County, Wisconsin, for example, the majority of the manure coming from the county's forty-one thousand dairy cows—more than 260 million gallons (984 million L) of manure per year—is spread on nearby grain fields.

WORDS IN CONTEXT

aeration

To supply something such as soil with air.

To help connect farmers who want to dispose of manure with people who want to receive it, some people participate in programs known as manure shares. These programs are often run by a conservation group, an agricultural advisory group, or some other group or agency devoted to helping farmers practice sustainable agriculture in ways that also provide economic benefits. They use mailing lists, sign-up sheets, and online posts to help all interested parties share information about what is available, what is needed, whether the manure is free, and whether the person providing the manure is willing to deliver it.

In many areas, however, livestock facilities generate far more manure than their local communities can absorb. In other words, there are simply too few individuals who want or need natural fertilizer in relation to how much manure is being produced there. (Many people prefer commercially manufactured fertilizers, which are manufactured using manipulated animal and vegetable ma-

AGRICULTURAL RUNOFF

Scientists and health experts are becoming increasingly concerned about agricultural practices that are unsustainable because of the serious damage they do to the environment. A significant amount of this damage is caused by agricultural runoff, which is water from farms—often contaminated with fertilizer and/or animal waste—that leaves the property because of rain, melting snow, or irrigation. According to the EPA, agricultural runoff is the number one pollutant of the nation's rivers and streams. In addition, studies suggest that roughly 20 million Americans a year are sickened by water contaminated with parasites, bacteria, or viruses, and a significant amount of these contaminants come from human and animal waste.

The problems associated with contaminated runoff can be particularly severe during periods of heavy rains or early spring melts because of the increase in water washing over the land. After one such period in 2009, 30 percent of the wells in a town in Brown County, Wisconsin, were found to be so contaminated by runoff containing animal waste that they were considered a serious risk to public health. One resident whose home water supply relied on such a well said at the time, "Sometimes it smells like a barn coming out of the faucet."

Katherine Harmon, "Mooo-ve That Manure: Agricultural Runoff a Spreading Public Health Issue," *News Blog, Scientific American*, September 18, 2009. https://blogs.scientificamerican.com.

nures, plant nutrients, and other materials.) When this occurs, even a well-run manure-share system is unsustainable.

Poor Health

Experts in sustainable agriculture say one way to address this imbalance is to limit the number of factory farms—and the number of animals on each farm—in a given area. This would reduce at least some of the impact of having too much manure in one place. Some environmentalists argue that factory farming should be abolished altogether because having too many animals housed in one place can so easily overwhelm the surrounding environment. In addition, they say, the more manure there is, the greater the likelihood that a manure-related accident will occur.

Experts note that it is also more difficult for factory farms to keep animals healthy because diseases spread more easily among large populations living in close quarters. For example, beef cattle kept in feedlots can be exposed to a variety of illnesses, most commonly respiratory diseases—but with hundreds or thousands of animals, it can be difficult to tell when one of them falls ill. Therefore, farmers typically try to prevent such outbreaks through the use of vaccinations and antibiotics.

Proponents of sustainable agriculture argue that a better way to prevent illnesses among beef cattle is to stop feeding them grain. Grain fattens the animals up more quickly for slaughter, but studies have shown that it can also increase their likelihood of getting sick. This is because grain does not have enough fiber for cattle, and too little fiber can cause digestive problems and stomach ulcers. These conditions can allow infectious and sometimes deadly bacteria to enter the cow's bloodstream.

Good Grazing Practices

Keeping animals healthy is a vital part of sustainable livestock practices. For this reason, many proponents of sustainable agriculture say that cattle should be allowed to graze in pastures rather than being fed grain or commercial foods. This change, food blogger Elizabeth Passarella says, would lead to better animal health. She writes, "They roam, they chew grass, they take naps in the pasture. That sort of thing. They eat the diet they were born to eat, which means they are healthier."[30]

In fact, scientists have discovered that certain types of plants can improve the way that cattle and sheep digest their food. For example, an enzyme in a type of clover increases cows' ability to utilize dietary protein, which in turn enables them to produce more milk. Given such benefits to animal health, the Grace Communications Foundation says that "truly sustainable livestock farming requires the use of a pasture-based system."[31]

Scientists also say that moving cows from pasture to pasture aids animal health. It allows the animals to eat a mix of grass and other pasture plants as well as trees with edible leaves and fruit. This is good not just for the animals but for the farm as well, because it leaves the natural environment intact. In a report on research into this issue, the University of Cambridge explains

Scientists say that moving cows from pasture to pasture aids animal health because it gives cows a more diverse diet. Allowing cows to graze in different pastures also helps keeps the land healthy because it avoids overuse.

that allowing animals to graze on land that mixes trees with forage "promotes healthy soil with better water retention (and less runoff), encourages predators of harmful animals, minimizes greenhouse gas emissions . . . reduces injury and stress in animals, improves welfare and encourages biodiversity using native shrubs and trees."[32]

Not Enough Land

But others say that a livestock system based on grazing is not sustainable either. In explaining why, James E. McWilliams, author of the book *Just Food: Where Locavores Get It Wrong and How We Can Truly Eat Responsibly*, says:

> It requires 2 to 20 acres to raise a cow on grass. If we raised all the cows in the United States on grass (all 100 million of them), cattle would require (using the figure of 10 acres per cow) almost half the country's land (and this figure excludes space needed for pastured chicken and pigs). A tract of land just larger than France has been carved out of the Brazilian rain forest and turned over to grazing cattle. Nothing about this is sustainable.[33]

A COMBINED APPROACH

Some scientists argue that the best way to make livestock production more sustainable—and to improve agricultural sustainability overall—is to combine plant and animal agriculture. Most farms (or ranches) focus on one or the other: growing crops or raising livestock. It was not always done this way—and these scientists believe that returning to the practice of side-by-side farming and livestock would benefit farms, animals, people, and the environment. Among the proponents of this change is the Union of Concerned Scientists (UCS), a nonprofit organization composed of scientists, engineers, and others dedicated to developing and implementing solutions to environmental problems.

Noting that factory farming ignores "the societal cost of pollution," the UCS points out that raising livestock and crops on the same property meets two needs at once. Manure from livestock can be used to fertilize the farm's crops, and cattle can graze on fields that are fallow (that is, standing idle). The group states that this combined approach to farming would have many benefits: "Crop and livestock reintegration can be accomplished on a regional basis or on individual farms; distributing animal operations throughout the Midwest would produce a range of benefits, from reduced nutrient pollution to enhanced soil fertility."

Union of Concerned Scientists, "Healthy Farm Practices: Integrating Crops and Livestock," September 27, 2016. www.ucsusa.org.

There are other reasons that grazing is unsustainable as well. According to the environmental group the Nature Conservancy, in North America between 30 percent and 70 percent of the roughly 775 million acres (314 million ha) of grazed land has been degraded by the grazing. In other words, there has been significant topsoil erosion, plant damage, and loss of biodiversity from what the group deems unsustainable land management that is "threatening the health and well-being of the people, plants, and animals that depend on these lands."[34]

So far there are no solutions to this problem. However, the Nature Conservancy and other environmental groups are working toward finding some. The Nature Conservancy says that among its goals related to damage caused by grazing are "developing tools and strategies that people can use to manage grazing lands toward improved condition" and "providing scientific evidence that these tools and methods work on the ground."[35]

There are also groups dedicated to supporting efforts related to the sustainability of beef, though experts disagree on how this term should be defined. Some say that sustainable beef is beef that is produced in ways that are environmentally sound, socially responsible, and economically viable. Others include the food value of the beef in the definition—like rancher Amanda Radke, who says, "To me, sustainable beef is that which is produced efficiently, packs the most nutrient punch and creates the least environmental impact."[36] One thing most people agree on is that when meat, egg, and milk production comes at the expense of animal and environmental health, it is simply not sustainable.

CHAPTER FIVE

Sustainable Agriculture and Climate

> **"Agriculture both contributes to climate change and is affected by climate change."**
>
> —European Environment Agency
>
> European Environment Agency, "Agriculture and Climate Change," 2015. www.eea.europa.eu.

The subjects of sustainable agriculture and climate change—a change in the earth's climate involving warmer average temperatures—are closely related for two reasons. First, agriculture is dependent on the weather, and warmer temperatures can have an adverse effect on growing crops. Second, scientists believe that agricultural practices contribute to climate change by increasing the greenhouse effect.

The greenhouse effect is vital to all life on earth because it is what keeps the planet from experiencing the same temperature extremes as the moon. The moon's temperature ranges from roughly 273°F (134°C) during the day to -244°F (-153°C) at night. More specifically, gases in the earth's atmosphere—which include carbon dioxide, methane, nitrogen oxide, and ozone—allow the atmosphere to act like a blanket, protecting the earth from the full force of the sun's energy while trapping enough of the earth's heat to keep the planet warm enough to make it habitable.

But the denser the gases, the more heat the atmosphere traps and the hotter the earth gets. This is why scientists are concerned about the many human activities that increase the amount of greenhouse gases in the atmosphere—and a significant number of these activities are related to farming. According to CGIAR (formerly the Consultative Group on International Agricultural Research)—a partnership of fifteen research centers around the world—the global food system is responsible for 33 percent of all greenhouse gas emissions related to human activity. The global food system includes everything related to growing crops, raising livestock, manufacturing products like fertilizers and pesticides, and storing, packaging, and transporting food.

Cheese is packaged and readied for shipment. The global food system—which includes growing crops; raising livestock; and manufacturing, packaging, and transporting farm products—contributes to greenhouse gas emissions and climate change.

A Long-Term Trend

Reliable records of scientific measurements show that the amount of greenhouse gases in the atmosphere contributed by all human activities increased by 35 percent from 1990 to 2010. Moreover, according to the EPA, in 2016 alone the amount of carbon dioxide—a greenhouse gas that can increase in the atmosphere as a result of certain farming activities related to soil management—rose by 3.4 parts per million. This is its fastest rise on record in a single year. And based on studies of core samples from polar ice caps, some scientists believe that the atmosphere has never had as much carbon dioxide as it has today.

Scientists also say the earth's temperature has never been as hot as it is today. In January 2017 several scientific bodies, including the World Meteorological Organization and the United States' National Oceanic and Atmospheric Administration (NOAA), publicly declared 2016 to be the hottest year on earth. They based their findings primarily on reliable records of global temperatures dating back to 1850. Such records also show that today's high temperatures are part of a long-term trend, whereby the average global temperature across land and ocean surface areas has been gradually getting warmer. For example, the NOAA reports that the average global temperature in the twentieth century was 55.2°F (12.9°C); the average global temperature in 2016 was 1.69°F (0.95°C) higher than this.

A difference of roughly one degree Celsius might not seem like a lot, but experts say it can have dramatic effects on the climate. According to Michael Carlowicz of the National Aeronautics and Space Administration, "A one-degree *global* change is significant because it takes a vast amount of heat to warm all the oceans, atmosphere, and land by that much. In the past, a one- to two-degree drop was all it took to plunge the Earth into the Little Ice Age. A five-degree drop was enough to bury a large part of North America under a towering mass of ice 20,000 years ago."[37]

Worldwide Efforts

Scientists say that if the current rise in the earth's temperature continues, it will lead to heat waves and droughts long enough

SUSTAINABLE IRRIGATION PRACTICES

Scientists have warned that sustained droughts are one possible outcome of continued warming of the earth. If that happens, lack of water could make farming unsustainable. For this reason, scientists and farmers are working on new methods of irrigation.

One such system is already in use on farms near Happy, Texas, where wells have been running dry for years. Farmers there are using pivot irrigators, also called waterwheels, to deliver water via spray nozzles at an average rate of just 1 inch (2.5 cm) per eight days. This system saves water but does not work well for all crops. For example, it provides enough water for cotton and sorghum but too little for corn and wheat.

Scientists working at an experimental farm near Amarillo, Texas, have been trying to reduce water usage without cutting back on the amount of water that actually reaches the plants. In one such system, a computer continuously monitors leaf moisture and overall plant health and then adjusts the amount of water going to the plants accordingly. Another idea being tested involves water that is delivered directly to each plant's roots underground. Both methods reduce wasted water. In discussing these methods, soil scientist Steve Evett says, "We are already seeing much less water used, and there is going to be less and less to use. Things will get harder and harder, but we can use technology to offset the drying for as long as we can."

Quoted in Charles Laurence, "US Farmers Fear the Return of the Dust Bowl," *Telegraph* (London), March 7, 2011. www.telegraph.co.uk.

and intense enough to disrupt the world's food supply. Therefore, they have worked for at least a decade to get policy makers involved in efforts to combat climate change, and in 2015 such efforts bore fruit. Specifically, representatives from 195 nations met at the United Nations Framework Convention on Climate Change in Paris, France, to hammer out an agreement—now known as the Paris Agreement—whereby countries could pledge to reduce their contributions to the greenhouse gases in the atmosphere by significant amounts. As of March 2017, 197 countries had become parties to this agreement (meaning they had agreed to abide by its terms), of which 148 subsequently ratified the agreement (made its terms legally binding). However, on June 1, 2017,

US president Donald Trump announced that the United States would pull out of the landmark global agreement. The only other countries that are not parties to this agreement are Nicaragua in Central America and Syria in the Middle East.

The Paris Agreement leaves it up to each party to decide how to reduce its emissions. However, the agreement requires nations to come up with detailed plans on how they will accomplish this so that they can report publicly every five years, begin-

US president Donald Trump announced in June 2017 that the United States would withdraw from the Paris Agreement. This landmark international agreement is aimed at reducing emissions that are contributing to climate change.

ning in 2023, on their progress. In guiding countries in these efforts, the agreement emphasizes the need to consider land use, particularly in regard to forests and agriculture. Duncan Marsh, director of international climate policy for the environmental group the Nature Conservancy, explains, "The agreement affirms the important role that ecosystems, biodiversity, and land use can play in reducing greenhouse gas emissions and helping communities and countries reduce risks and adapt to climate change impacts. It also promotes sustainable management of land, which can range from conserving and restoring forests to improving agriculture."[38] In addition, a major conference on climate change in November 2016 in Marrakech, Morocco, held in support of the Paris Agreement, featured at least eighty sessions on subjects related to how agricultural practices impact the environment.

A New Willingness

This willingness on the part of diplomats, politicians, and other policy makers to consider the connection between climate change and agriculture is a relatively new development. Experts on climate change report that at the first global climate summit in 1992, people rarely talked about agriculture. Then roughly ten years ago, the subject of how deforestation was affecting the climate began to come up at such gatherings, and because much of this deforestation was related to farming, the discussion eventually turned to agriculture. Now, nearly 80 percent of the parties to the Paris Agreement have said they will alter agricultural practices as part of their efforts to achieve their emissions goals. In addition, over 90 percent have said they will make changes in regard to the ways that forests and other types of land are affected by farming.

Farmers too are more open than in years past to new policies that address climate change, because they fear the threat to their livelihood that continued warming would pose. According to Ernie Shea of Solutions from the Land, most farmers know what might await them if scientists' warnings are right. He says, "Drought impacts, flooding, higher nighttime temperatures affecting pollination, new weeds, invasive species. There's an awareness in the agriculture community that we're at risk and we're not as resilient as we need to be."[39] However, not all farmers are willing to take this risk seriously enough to change their traditional agricultural practices. Some do not believe that the climate will ever change that dramatically. Others do not believe that their own actions will have a bearing on how bad the climate gets.

Environmentalists have found that the best way to counter such resistance is to emphasize the fact that adopting climate-friendly agricultural practices can benefit farmers as much as it can benefit the environment: The adoption of sustainable practices can make farms more productive. As Shea explains, "People are turned off by the climate change conversation. Once you get into a conversation about improving productivity, you can get into a conversation about co-benefits."[40] This is also the position taken by Thomas Driscoll of the National Farmers Union, one of the largest farm groups in the United States, who notes, "Doing the right thing for the climate can save farmers money."[41]

Soil Carbon

One way that farmers can help both the climate and their farms is to ensure that their soil retains its carbon. Soil contains carbon and other minerals as well as a variety of living things, such as microbes—tiny single-cell organisms that include bacteria and fungi. If the carbon disappears, the microbes cannot survive—and without microbes the soil becomes dirt, a sterile substrate in which many plants cannot thrive.

There are several reasons why carbon might disappear. As the Ecological Society of America reports, "Carbon can remain stored in soils for millennia, or be quickly released back into the atmosphere. Climatic conditions, natural vegetation, soil texture, and drainage all affect

WORDS IN CONTEXT

substrate

The layer or surface where an organism grows and/or obtains its nourishment.

ENCOURAGING PESTS AND DISEASES

Climate change can adversely affect attempts to control pests and diseases in crops. Scientific studies have shown that pesticides generally do not work as well in warm climates as cold climates. Droughts can also make pesticides less effective because long periods of direct sunlight degrade the chemicals in pesticides. Moreover, higher levels of carbon dioxide can lower the amount of nitrogen in leaves, which in turn drives insects to eat more of the leaves in order to meet their nitrogen needs. Higher temperatures also allow insects that would normally die during the winter to survive longer. Higher temperatures and higher levels of carbon dioxide can benefit certain kinds of disease-causing organisms as well, expanding their range and fueling their growth. All of this means that climate change can be responsible for creating insect and disease infestations that are severe enough to threaten agricultural sustainability.

the amount and length of time carbon is stored."[42] However, the main way to keep carbon in the soil is to keep it from being exposed to air, because this can cause carbon to oxidize. That is, carbon plus oxygen becomes carbon dioxide, a greenhouse gas, and once this happens the carbon dioxide goes from the soil into the atmosphere.

Indeed, Rattan Lal of Ohio State University's Carbon Management and Sequestration Center reports that cultivation over the centuries has caused the earth's soil to lose between 50 percent and 70 percent of its carbon, and much of this carbon oxidized and went into the atmosphere. Therefore, Lal says, "soils of the world must be part of any agenda to address climate change, as well as food and water security. I think there is now a general awareness of soil carbon, an awareness that soil isn't just a medium for plant growth."[43]

Cover Cropping

Studies have also shown that an estimated 86 billion tons (78 billion metric tons) of carbon have been released from the soil because of tilling. Tilling involves turning the soil to make it easier to add soil amendments, remove weeds and roots, and seed new crops. Farmers who want to prevent carbon from leaving their soil are careful not to over-till their soil prior to planting. Others might go one step further by practicing no-till farming. Also known as direct drilling, this practice typically involves using a seed drill to put the seed directly into the soil and stubble left behind by the previous crop. Thus, the soil is left largely undisturbed, and as Bruce McCarl, an agricultural economist at Texas A&M University, notes, "anything that reduces soil disturbance increases carbon storage."[44]

WORDS IN CONTEXT

fallow

Used to refer to farmland that has been tilled but left unsown, often temporarily.

Another way that farmers can keep carbon from leaving their fields is to practice cover cropping. This is done during times when the fields are fallow, such as between a fall harvest and the end of winter. At such times, farmers can plant an extra crop—typically one rich in nitrogen, like alfalfa—without necessarily intending for it to grow to maturity. This is because its main purpose is to protect the soil from erosion (which allows carbon into the air) and to replenish the nutrients the soil lost to the recently harvested crop. Farmers can also replenish soil carbon in fallow fields by allowing animals to graze there. The animals' trampling not only compacts the soil (the opposite of tilling it) but presses dead plant matter into it, thereby "feeding" the soil microorganisms.

Methane

However, animals also contribute to climate change because they produce greenhouse gases via their digestive and respiratory systems. In fact, livestock—particularly cattle, buffalo, sheep, and goats—are among the main sources of methane and nitrous oxide emissions. Cattle account for one-third of all greenhouse gases produced by livestock globally, while pigs are the source of half of the world's methane emissions.

Plants can be sources of greenhouse gases as well. In fact, rice paddies are among the most significant sources of methane because the warm, waterlogged soil required to grow rice encourages the formation of methane by microbes known as

The traditional method of growing rice in a flooded field (pictured) releases large amounts of methane into the atmosphere. Researchers say that other methods of growing rice can reduce methane emissions.

methanogens. Moreover, the warmer the weather and the more carbon dioxide there is in the atmosphere, the more methane the rice releases into the atmosphere. Specifically, methane from rice is responsible for 1.5 percent of the total greenhouse gas emissions. While this might not sound like a lot, scientists note that in terms of negative effects, methane is more than thirty times more harmful than carbon dioxide.

WORDS IN CONTEXT

methanogens
Methane-producing bacteria.

However, there are ways that farmers can reduce the amount of methane that growing rice produces while also improving their productivity and profits. Specifically, most rice is grown in flooded fields, but this is not absolutely necessary. Researchers with the World Resources Institute, a global research organization focused on sustaining natural resources, explain, "Almost any farming method that reduces or interrupts the period of flooding can reduce methane."[45] For example, the water level in a rice field can be reduced midseason so that the water barely covers the roots, a practice known as a drawdown. Or instead of growing the rice in a flooded field, the rice can be grown in rows of raised soil beds separated by shallow trenches or furrows. Rather than flooding the entire field, only the furrows would be flooded to provide rice crops with water. The researchers say that such measures not only "reduce rice-growing emissions dramatically" but can "conserve water and . . . boost yields."[46]

Working Together

There are many other ways that farmers and others involved in the agriculture industry (such as fertilizer producers) can reduce their contribution to greenhouse gases. For example, they can use polluting machinery and vehicles more efficiently or even switch to more fuel-efficient versions. They can buy supplies and sell produce or products locally in order to avoid transporting these items over long distances. However, such activities do not necessarily increase profits or productivity.

Experts on both climate change and sustainable agriculture are well aware of the economic needs of farmers. In fact, the CGIAR-sponsored Commission on Sustainable Agriculture and Climate Change, made up of experts on global climate change, agriculture, and food security, has stated, "Agricultural sustainability hinges on development and uptake of farming techniques that simultaneously deliver robust yields and incomes, climate resilience and greenhouse gas mitigation."[47] As an example of how the commission recommends this be accomplished, its report titled "Achieving Food Security in the Face of Climate Change" points to efforts being made in Vietnam. Rice growers there are learning ways to lower the levels of methane and nitrous oxide in their rice paddies while increasing their yields. They are also learning to cut down on overuse of fertilizers, pesticides, and irrigation so that they use only as much as their fields require.

The commission recommends that farmers and scientists work together as much as possible to reduce any harmful effects of agriculture on the environment while also intensifying agricultural production in sustainable ways. It also points out that governments throughout the world have roles to play in promoting sustainable agriculture in the face of climate change. As examples of how policy makers can support efforts in this regard, the commission suggests finding ways to reward farmers for adopting beneficial farming systems, supporting agricultural research programs, encouraging innovations, and offering programs and financial aid that will help people whose farms are at the most risk of being threatened by climate change. It also calls for specific programs and policies to assist populations that are the most vulnerable to climate change and food insecurity.

Many experts are concerned about the security of the food system in the face of climate change. They worry that if global warming continues, farmers will be unable to adapt to a world where heat and drought have become the norm, and as a result there will not be nearly enough food for the growing global population. Others, however, are confident that farmers and scientists will find ways to provide a sustainable food system in the face of worsening climate conditions. For example, the US Department of Agriculture states:

> Challenges to a sustainable, global food system that will carry us through the coming years and into the next century are daunting. However, we have access to a storehouse of tools with which to work: a diverse agricultural knowledge base; interdisciplinary research and expertise; cutting-edge technology applications; and a global communication system with which to share information.[48]

Introduction: The Role of Science

1. Quoted in Mike Adams, "America's Breadbasket Aquifer Running Dry," *Natural News* (blog), March 10, 2011. www.naturalnews.com.
2. Adams, "America's Breadbasket Aquifer Running Dry."
3. UC Davis Agricultural Sustainability Institute, "What Is Sustainable Agriculture?" http://asi.ucdavis.edu.
4. Grace Communications Foundation, "Sustainable Crop Production," 2017. www.sustainabletable.org.
5. Ian Chubb, "The Role of Science in Sustainable Agriculture," transcript, November 15, 2012. www.chiefscientist.gov.au.

Chapter One: Science and the Sustainability Movement

6. Quoted in Leon Hesser, *The Man Who Fed the World*, excerpts, SeedQuest Forum, 2006. www.seedquest.com.
7. Justin Gillis, "Norman Borlaug, Plant Scientist Who Fought Famine, Dies at 97," *New York Times*, September 13, 2009. www.nytimes.com.
8. Henry I. Miller, "Norman Borlaug: The Genius Behind the Green Revolution," *Forbes*, January 18, 2012. www.forbes.com.
9. Miller, "Norman Borlaug."
10. International Food Policy Research Institute, "Green Revolution: Curse or Blessing?," Oregon State University, 2002. https://oregonstate.edu.
11. Phillip A. Sharp and Alan Leshner, "We Need a New Green Revolution," *New York Times*, January 4, 2016. www.nytimes.com.
12. Sharp and Leshner, "We Need a New Green Revolution."
13. Quoted in *UDaily* (Univ. of Delaware), "UD's Wisser Receives USDA Grant to Study Genetic Barriers in Corn," November 15, 2011. www1.udel.edu.
14. Richard Hamilton, "Agriculture's Sustainable Future: Breeding Better Crops," *Scientific American*, June 1, 2009. www.scientificamerican.com.

Chapter Two: Promoting Biodiversity

15. Sami Grover, "Diversity Is Key to Sustainable Farming, So Why's It So Damn Hard?," TreeHugger, May 6, 2011. www.treehugger.com.

16. Center for Health and the Global Environment, Harvard T.H. Chan School of Public Health, "Biodiversity and Agriculture." www.chgeharvard.org.

17. Quoted in University of California–Davis, "Why Insect Pests Love Monocultures, and How Plant Diversity Could Change That," ScienceDaily, October 12, 2016. www.sciencedaily.com.

18. Quoted in SeedWorld, "Seed Industry Calls for Global Coalition to Strengthen Food Security," 2016. http://seedworld.com.

19. Quoted in Greg Breining, "In the Race to Save Species, GMOs Are Coming to Nature," *Ensia*, August 24, 2015. https://ensia.com.

20. Quoted in Peter J. Jacques and Jessica Racine Jacques, "Monocropping Cultures into Ruin," *Sustainability*, November 7, 2012. www.mdpi.com.

21. Quoted in Joseph Mercola, "Photographic Adventure Reveals the Frightening Deadness of Genetically Engineered Corn Field," Mercola, January 1, 2013. http://articles.mercola.com.

Chapter Three: Fighting Pests

22. Quoted in Kieron Monks, "Armyworm Invasion Destroys Crops in Southern Africa," CNN, January 24, 2017. www.cnn.com.

23. Quoted in Matthew Hill, "Alien Armyworm Invading Africa May Reach Asia, Mediterranean," *Chicago Tribune*, February 6, 2017. www.chicagotribune.com.

24. Quoted in Jason Bittel, "Second Silent Spring? Bird Declines Linked to Popular Pesticides," *National Geographic*, July 9, 2014. http://news.nationalgeographic.com.

25. Kenneth Wilson, "Armyworms Are Wreaking Havoc in Southern Africa. Why It's a Big Deal," Conversation, February 12, 2017. http://theconversation.com.

26. Quoted in Tom Philpott, "New Monsanto Spray Kills Bugs by Messing with Their Genes," *Mother Jones*, August 19, 2015. www.motherjones.com.

27. Quoted in Brenda Wawa, "Scientists Tackle Deadly Fall Armyworm Infestation Devastating Maize in Southern Africa," CIMMYT, February 23, 2017. www.cimmyt.org.
28. Quoted in Food Journal and Food, Nutrition & Science, "Why Do Farmers Spray Chemicals on Crops?," March 12, 2015. www.foodnutritionscience.com.

Chapter Four: Livestock Practices

29. Quoted in University of Cambridge, "Sustainable Livestock Production Is Possible," September 25, 2013. www.cam.ac.uk.
30. Elizabeth Passerella, "Grass-Fed Versus Grain-Fed Beef: What's the Difference and Why Does It Matter?," *The Kitchn* (blog), May 12, 2009. www.thekitchn.com.
31. Grace Communications Foundation, "Sustainable Livestock Husbandry," 2017. www.sustainabletable.org.
32. University of Cambridge, "Sustainable Livestock Production Is Possible."
33. James E. McWilliams, "The Myth of Sustainable Meat," *New York Times*, April 12, 2012. www.nytimes.com.
34. Nature Conservancy, "North America Agriculture: Sustainable Grazing," 2017. www.nature.org.
35. Nature Conservancy, "North America Agriculture."
36. Amanda Radke, "What Is Sustainable Beef?," *Beef Daily* (blog), *Beef*, October 23, 2012. www.beefmagazine.com.

Chapter Five: Sustainable Agriculture and Climate

37. Michael Carlowicz, "Global Temperatures," NASA Earth Observatory. https://earthobservatory.nasa.gov.
38. Quoted in Nature Conservancy, "Climate Change: The Paris Agreement," 2017. www.nature.org.
39. Quoted in Georgina Gustin, "2017: Agriculture Begins to Tackle Its Role in Climate Change," InsideClimate News, January 4, 2017. https://insideclimatenews.org.
40. Quoted in Gustin, "2017."
41. Quoted in Gustin, "2017."
42. Quoted in *TreePeople Blog*, "5 Reasons We Can't Live Without Soil," May 6, 2015. https://blog.treepeople.org.

43. Quoted in Judith D. Schwartz, "Soil as Carbon Storehouse: New Weapon in Climate Fight?," *Yale Environment 360*, March 4, 2014. http://e360.yale.edu.
44. Quoted in David Biello, "Combating Climate Change: Farming Out Global Warming Solutions," *Scientific American*, May 25, 2007. www.scientificamerican.com.
45. Tim Searchinger and Richard Waite, "More Rice, Less Methane," World Resources Institute, December 16, 2014. www.wri.org.
46. Searchinger and Waite, "More Rice, Less Methane."
47. Commission on Sustainable Agriculture and Climate Change, "Achieving Food Security in the Face of Climate Change," November 2011. https://cgspace.cgiar.org.
48. US Department of Agriculture, "Tracing the Evolution of Organic/Sustainable Agriculture," May 2007. www.nal.usda.gov.

FIND OUT MORE

Books

Joel K. Borne Jr., *The End of Plenty: The Race to Feed a Crowded World*. New York: Norton, 2015.

Nancy F. Castaldo, *The Story of Seeds: From Mendel's Garden to Your Plate, and How There's More of Less to Eat Around the World*. New York: Houghton Mifflin, 2016.

Carol Hand, *Sustainable Agriculture*. Minneapolis, MN: Essential Library, 2016.

Jan Reynolds, *Cycle of Rice: A Story of Sustainable Farming*. New York: Lee & Low, 2013.

Caitlin Shetterly, *Modified: GMOs and the Threat to Our Food, Our Land, Our Future*. New York: Putnam, 2016.

Stone Barns Center for Food and Agriculture, *Letters to a Young Farmer: On Food, Farming, and Our Future*. New York: Princeton Agricultural Press, 2017.

Lisa A. Wroble, *Starving: Can We Feed Everyone?* New York: Enslow, 2016.

Internet Sources

David Biello, "Genetically Modified Crop on the Loose and Evolving in U.S. Midwest," *Scientific American*, August 6, 2010. www.scientificamerican.com/article/genetically-modified-crop/.

Victoria Wilson, "How the Growth of Monoculture Crops Is Destroying Our Planet and Still Leaving Us Hungry," One Green Planet, October 17, 2014. www.onegreenplanet.org/animalsand nature/monoculture-crops-environment.

Websites

EcoCentric (www.gracelinks.org/blog). Provided by the Grace Communications Foundation, this blog provides stories, articles, and other information related to food, water, and energy sustainability.

Modern Farmer (http://modernfarmer.com). Associated with an agricultural magazine, this site provides information related to how food gets from farm to table.

National Young Farmers Coalition (www.youngfarmers.org). This site provides information and support for young farmers, along with a blog on farm-related subjects.

Seed Stock (http://seedstock.com). This site provides news and information related to sustainable food systems.

UC Davis College of Agricultural and Environmental Sciences (www.caes.ucdavis.edu). This site provides articles and other information related to agricultural and environmental sciences, as well as about studying these subjects at the University of California–Davis.

US Department of Agriculture (www.usda.gov). This site provides a wealth of information about farming practices and agricultural issues in the United States.

Virtual Grange (www.virtualgrange.org). Managed by the Stone Barns Center for Food and Agriculture, this site provides farming-related information and an online community for beginning farmers.

INDEX

PICTURE CREDITS

Cover: Shutterstock.com/Daxiao Productions

6: Maury Aaseng

11: Shutterstock/Budimir Jevtic

14: Associated Press

18: Associated Press

23: Clouds Hill Imaging/Science Source

27: Shutterstock.com/Tom Ruethai

30: Shutterstock/Gorilla Images

34: Shutterstock.com/Mikhail Kochiev

36: Minden Pictures

41: Maury Aaseng

46: West Jim/Sipa/Newscom

49: iStockphoto.com/Simply Creative Photography

53: iStockphoto/RJ Seymour

57: iStockphoto/leezsnow

60: Christy Bowe/Polaris/Newscom

65: Shutterstock/Chung Toan Co

ABOUT THE AUTHOR

Patricia D. Netzley is the author of more than seventy nonfiction books for children, teens, and adults on a variety of subjects, including environmental issues and environmental literature. She also writes novels for young adults.

SEP 1 4 2017